TOG THE RIBBER
or Granny's Tale

For Jean and her grandchildren

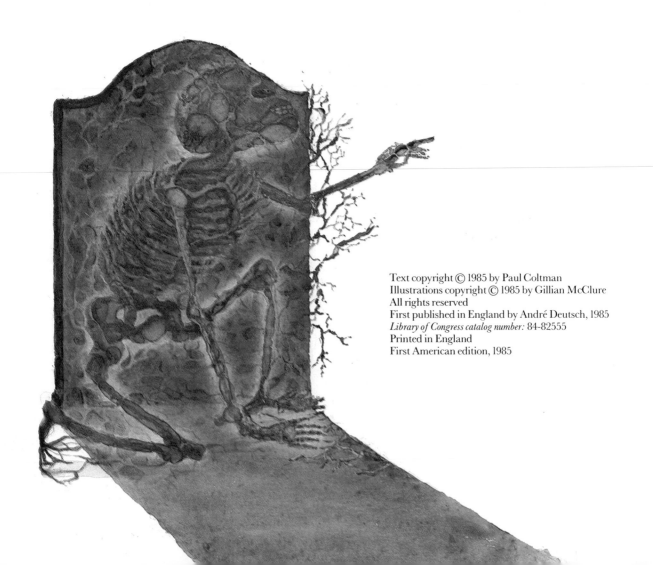

TOG THE RIBBER
or Granny's Tale

Poem by Paul Coltman
Illustrations by Gillian McClure

FARRAR STRAUS GIROUX
New York

our granny had a dreadful flight.
And that is why her hair is white.
And that is why she don't speak right.

 shuddud in the glavering goom
as homing through the only wood
I skibbed and teetered past Tog's tomb.

he path went skinny by a brook
where heaved an owly-headed tree
and on its mozzy trunk a hook.

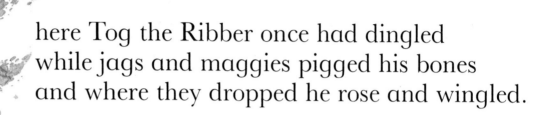here Tog the Ribber once had dingled
while jags and maggies pigged his bones
and where they dropped he rose and wingled.

is shrieklich ghost and howling bones
had driven men crazy far and wild;

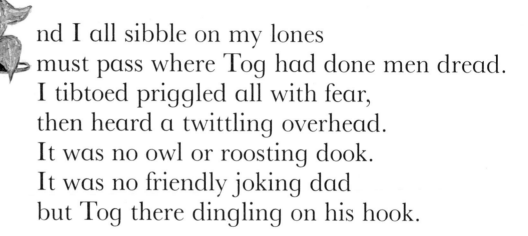

nd I all sibble on my lones
must pass where Tog had done men dread.
I tibtoed priggled all with fear,
then heard a twittling overhead.
It was no owl or roosting dook.
It was no friendly joking dad
but Tog there dingling on his hook.

shrikked, "Oh woly, woly me!"
as Tog begun to clumber down,
unhooking arm and leg and knee.
He did, but then his blackbone hitched.
I heard him swore. He could not move,

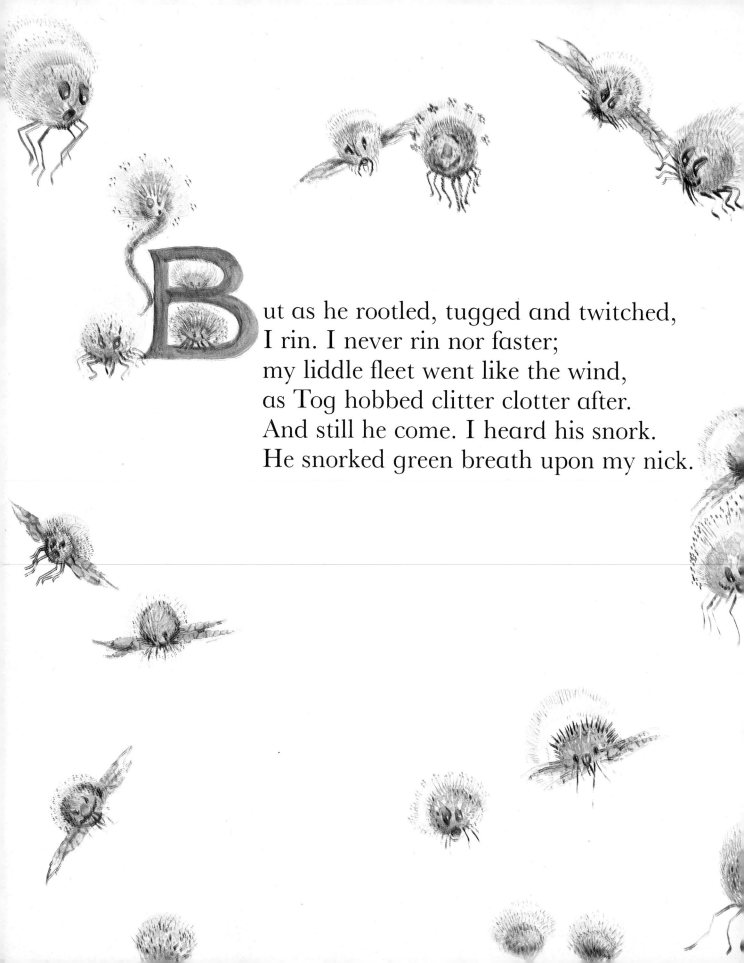

But as he rootled, tugged and twitched,
I rin. I never rin nor faster;
my liddle fleet went like the wind,
as Tog hobbed clitter clotter after.
And still he come. I heard his snork.
He snorked green breath upon my nick.

I rin. I rin. He seemed to walk.
But still he come. I felt his titch.
His shankle tried to trib me up.

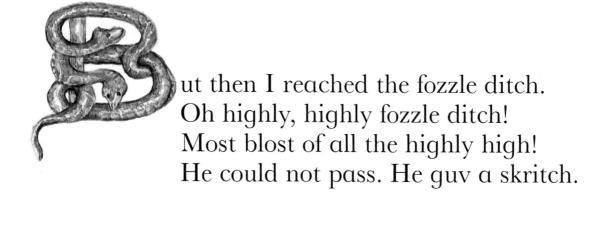

But then I reached the fozzle ditch.
Oh highly, highly fozzle ditch!
Most blost of all the highly high!
He could not pass. He guv a skritch.

And as I twiddled round to look,
I saw Tog's grozzly heap of bones
go staggling back towards their hook.

ome, home! My mam a tear she shed.
My daddling kussed his liddle girl
and popped me in my cosly bed.

ut ever since on owly nights
if I should hear the grunting wind,
I have to sleep all round with lights.

nd that is why gran fears the night.
And that is why her hair is white.
And that is why she don't speak right."